Original title:
Stumped for Sonnets

Copyright © 2025 Creative Arts Management OÜ
All rights reserved.

Author: Rosalie Bradford
ISBN HARDBACK: 978-1-80567-305-7
ISBN PAPERBACK: 978-1-80567-604-1

Whims of Words Unwritten

In a world where rhymes do dance,
My thoughts take a chance and prance.
They trip on letters, fall on 'muse',
Tumble like socks, no sense to lose.

The pen's a wand that won't comply,
It flicks and flutters, oh my, oh my!
Carpets of paper, thoughts take flight,
But where they land? Not quite in sight.

The Agony of Abandoned Artistry

My canvas waits with a sigh so deep,
Colors untamed, in shadows they creep.
The brush feels heavy, stuck in the drawer,
Like socks in laundry, lost evermore.

Each poem planned is a joke on me,
With punchlines hidden like a lost key.
I laugh at the clock, tick-tock, tick-tock,
While my ideas walk like a chicken's flock.

Contemplations in the Chasm

In the abyss where muses hide,
I wave a flag, there's nowhere to bide.
Thoughts echo back with a silly cheer,
"Why write now? Just have another beer!"

Each empty page is a punchline missed,
A writing prompt that quietly hissed.
I juggle with words like a clown at a fair,
But all I produce is a blank, empty stare.

Procrastination's Poetic Plight

The desk is a mess, a chaotic scene,
Vintage cups with tea stains, quite the sheen.
The muse is playing hide and seek,
    Cackling softly, oh so sleek.

I wander off to see what's on TV,
The world of writing seems too heavy for me.
An epic saga of getting nowhere,
With laughs and giggles floating in the air.

Shadows of an Unwritten Verse

A paper blank as winter's night,
With thoughts that dance just out of sight.
I tap my pen in sheer dismay,
Where have my dreams all run away?

The rhyme is hiding, playing coy,
My mind's a maze, devoid of joy.
A fleeting line slips through my grip,
Like ice cream melting from my lip.

With every riddle comes a yawn,
Excuses fade just like the dawn.
I juggle words, a clown on stage,
But all I scribble feels like page.

So here I muse in silly plight,
With shadows dancing in the light.
Perhaps a laugh will break the chain,
And spark a sonnet in my brain.

A Canvas of Unformed Dreams

A canvas stretched, so wide and bare,
With colors lost, a painter's glare.
Ideas drift like clouds in air,
Yet brush meets canvas, just a stare.

I hunt for muses, high and low,
While blocked thoughts laugh, "You've got no flow!"
A blankness stares, it mocks my fear,
"Add some splashes, Guernica dear!"

Crumpled papers strew my floor,
Each failed attempt, a phantom score.
Brush in hand, I fumble and slip,
And yet, I smile, I love this trip.

Oh, paint the sun and shade the moon,
I'll shake my fist and dance a tune.
Through playful jabs and joyful screams,
I'll fill my canvas with wild dreams.

Stalling at the Stanza's Edge

Here at the cliff where verses tease,
The wind of thoughts is just a breeze.
I tiptoe close, I peek and lean,
Will words emerge, or stay unseen?

A cat who ponders where to leap,
My pen lies still, it starts to creep.
The page a chasm waiting wide,
For silly jokes I'll try to hide.

Each stanza's edge, a wobbly walk,
My mind's a garden void of talk.
I chase the rhythm, seek the rhyme,
Yet here I sit, it's stalling time.

But laughter bubbles, tickles too,
As thoughts like bubbles float on through.
I'll scribble nonsense, call it art,
For in this zany fun, I'll start!

The Pause Before the Pen Falls

Before the pen begins to dance,
I take a moment, seize my chance.
I ponder life, its silly ways,
And how it teases through the days.

The silence grows, a ticking clock,
My brain is stuck, under a rock.
Yet chuckles bubble from my chest,
In waiting pause, I feel the jest.

A blank sheet shouts its silent plea,
"Come paint your humor, set me free!"
With goofy thoughts, I'll start to scrawl,
And let the laughter take the fall.

So here I sit, with giggles tight,
As inspiration takes its flight.
The pen is ready, let it roll,
We'll weave our tales, enjoy the stroll.

Half-Formed Fantasies

In a garden of thoughts, they twist and they roam,
Muffins wear hats, and sock puppets foam.
A cat with a mustache recites lines of cheer,
While the clock sings a tune that no one can hear.

A duck in a bowtie leads ducks with a map,
They waddle through dreams, what a splendid mishap!
Jellybeans dance to a tune made of guff,
And laughter erupts—who's ever had enough?

The Struggle Between Silence and Song

The cat tries to sing, but it sounds like a howl,
As the mouse wears a crown and begins to scowl.
Fish in a bowl keep their lips tightly sealed,
While frogs in a chorus go wild with zeal.

A tree hums a tune to the breeze's delight,
But the squirrels just snooze, they're not in the fight.
In the end, the wind whispers sweet nonsense anew,
While the sun shakes its head at the hullabaloo.

The Delicate Dance of a Dubious Dream

A pancake pirouettes with a syrup hat,
Ballet shoes sprout from a engaged chitchat.
The room spins around like a speedboat gone mad,
While the sausage rolls laugh at the antics they've had.

A pickle in tights takes the stage with a flair,
As the crowd of the condiments gasps in despair.
But let not the madness cause anyone fright,
For the giggles of joy bloom bright in the night.

Riddles in the Realm of Rhythm

What hops on the beat but can't hold a tune?
A frog on a drum, dancing under the moon.
Or what jumps with flair in a comical stew?
A chicken in tap shoes, can you guess who?

A jester in stripes spins a tale lopsided,
While whispers of giggles make minds feel divided.
In this land of oddities, laughter is king,
Where riddles abound, and the silliness sings.

The Wane of Wistful Whispers

A phrase once sparkled like a star,
Now it drowses, resting far.
The muse is taking an extended nap,
Leaving words in a sleepy trap.

Once I dreamed of brilliant rhymes,
Now I fumble, wasting times.
The pen trembles, I stare blankly,
My thoughts drift off, most frankly.

Ideas mingle in a swirl,
A jumble, an unfurling twirl.
Whispers laugh at my quiet plight,
As laughter fades into the night.

Oh, for a phrase to light the spark,
Instead, I bask in this dark park.
The wane of whispers, much too clear,
And yet I jest—ah, never fear!

The Phoenix of the Procrastinator

A phoenix rises, in delay's embrace,
With wings of wishes, at a sluggish pace.
Its flames flicker, a flick of doubt,
Burning bright, but not much clout.

The clock ticks by, as I sit and muse,
A dance of distraction, delightful ruse.
With cups of coffee, I take my stand,
But do my best with a half-done plan.

Ideas flutter, then lazily flop,
Chasing the muse, but she takes a hop.
I giggle at fire that won't ignite,
While teasing the spark hidden from sight.

A procrastinator's fate is grim,
Yet I chuckle, only on a whim.
For every phoenix of delay and dream,
Is a laugh, bursting, a brilliant gleam!

A Drought of Dreamy Diction

Words once danced upon the page,
Now they hide, lost in a cage.
A drought has settled, dry and fast,
I ponder phrases that just won't last.

The poet's heart is light and airy,
Yet here I fumble, feeling hairy.
Dreamy diction, where have you fled?
Leaving just a quill with dread.

I search for gems in tangled thought,
But find only jokes that I forgot.
A laughter echoes, so absurd,
As meaning fades without a word.

Still, in this drought, I'll make a jest,
At silly lines that fail the test.
For when the rain of words does stop,
It's laughs and giggles that take the top!

The Limitations of Languid Lines

Languid lines, they creep and crawl,
Like whispers heard in a fading hall.
They stretch too much, they slack too wide,
In their drumming, ideas hide.

Beneath the surface, phrases sleep,
While giggles bubble, oh so deep.
Their limitations make me sigh,
Yet every chuckle makes thoughts fly.

A lazy cat upon a chair,
Is this the muse? I see it there!
Inspired by naps, a dream so faint,
They float away—my own complaint.

Though languid lines may steal the show,
In their sluggishness, the humor flows.
For every limit draws a grin,
When laughter blooms, the heart will win!

The Silence of Singed Sentences

A pen that sputters, a word on fire,
The ink is laughing, my thoughts conspire.
Sentences dance, but the rhythm's off,
They trip and tumble, I can't help but scoff.

The paper's charred, but the jokes still spread,
I scribble wild tales that dance in my head.
But every attempt, a frizzle and pop,
Like popcorn kernels just longing to stop.

There's humor in chaos, a giggle in pain,
As I chase quirky stanzas, again and again.
The laughter erupts like a geyser at night,
In the silence of singed, where wrong feels so right.

With every mishap, I smile with glee,
Who knew my failings would set my words free?
So here's to the letters that never quite fit,
In the silence of singed, we find our wit.

The Brocade of Burdened Beliefs

Threads of thought, all tangled and torn,
Each belief a pattern, yet I feel so worn.
The fabric of wisdom frays at the seam,
Brocade of burden, or so it would seem.

I stitch with humor, a patchwork of laughs,
Weaving together my absurd little gaffes.
The weight of convictions brings one to tears,
But playful quips drown out all my fears.

In this frenetic quilt of wobbly truth,
A snicker erupts – oh, the folly of youth!
My snags and my gaffes, they dance like a twirl,
As the brocade of beliefs begins to unfurl.

With laughter as needle, I sew and I patch,
Turning burdens to fun, an unlikely match.
In the warmth of this fabric, we all can unite,
In the brocade of burdened, we find pure delight.

Conundrums in the Chaos of Creation

In the chaos of thought, where mischief resides,
A conundrum awaits, where humor collides.
Brushes and pencils, a whirlwind of fun,
I sketch out my worries, a whimsical run.

The canvas is crowded, ideas in knots,
With each stroke I ponder, and twist through the slots.
What should be a masterpiece, melds into a joke,
A landscape of nonsense, my palette awoke.

With giggles I ponder these puzzles so bright,
The chaos of creation, a curious sight.
Each blunder a treasure, each slip brings a cheer,
In conundrums of art, I shed every fear.

So dance with your doubts, let them take flight,
Amidst the commotion, find reasons to write.
For the joy is in making, let laughter unfurl,
In the chaos of creation, a beautiful swirl.

Echoes in the Empty Page

Once my quill danced, now it's still,
Ideas hide, I blame the thrill.
Pages whisper, secrets fade,
Where's that spark I thought I made?

I search for words in every nook,
Looking for that magic hook.
But every thought just runs away,
Seems they're off on holiday!

My mind's a circus, clowns abound,
Juggling thoughts that won't be found.
I grin and laugh at my plight,
Wishing ideas would take flight.

Between the lines, I hear them giggle,
Puns and jokes that make me wiggle.
Oh, to capture thoughts so sly,
But they just wink and wave goodbye!

A Riddle Wrapped in Rhyme

What is tricky, sly, and neat?
A puzzling dance on paper's sheet.
Each word a twist, a playful jest,
But answers hide, it's quite a test.

The rhyme does hop, the meter slips,
It flips and flops, then takes some trips.
With winks and nudges, it confounds,
Laughter echoes all around.

Is it a riddle or just me?
I scratch my head, slightly with glee.
Two left feet in a wordy ball,
As I stumble, I hear them call.

Oh puzzling friend with tricks to share,
Tickle my brain, show me you care.
In this game of wordy chase,
I trip and fall, then laugh with grace!

Fragments of a Fading Muse

Where did my muse go, I beseech?
She danced away, just out of reach.
Left me with crumbs, a tease, a wink,
And now I sit here, forced to think.

I chase her shadow through the night,
She giggles softly, what a sight!
In fragments scattered, chaos reigns,
Searching for something that remains.

Ideas flutter like lost leaves,
Each one too quick for me to seize.
In this merry game of cat and mouse,
I laugh at how she's slipped my house.

But oh dear muse, come back again,
Let's trade our secrets, sip some gin.
In this strange dance of hope and play,
I'll chase your fragments every day!

The Silence Between Stanzas

In the quiet, a ticklish breeze,
Words play hide and seek with trees.
The silence whispers, "What's the plan?"
But my mind's clear as a rusty pan.

Each stanza pauses with a sigh,
Wondering if it's time to fly.
But somehow they just sit and chew,
A noodle that forgot its brew.

Oh, the quiet is rich with dreams,
Yet every thought slips from my seams.
With laughter dancing in the air,
The silence giggles without a care.

So here I sit, pen in my hand,
Trying to understand this land.
In laughter, silence finds its grace,
And I just grin at this blank space!

Transitions of Turmoil and Tranquility

In the chaos of a busy mind,
You could swear a squirrel's there to unwind.
Thoughts flip-flop like a hapless fish,
Endless ideas, but none to polish.

Between laughter and despair's embrace,
Jokes tumble out, yet there's no grace.
With each failed rhyme, a chuckle grows,
A dance of chaos that nobody knows.

In tranquility, brief moments reside,
Like socks paired up with a dash of pride.
Yet turmoil finds its quirky play,
Turning silence into a comedy ballet.

In the end, who can say what's right?
A sonnet's a mess, a glorious sight.
With every stumble, we find our wit,
In a tangle of words, we just won't quit.

Weathered Pages and Worn Words

Old tomes whisper tales of yore,
Ink smudges dance like a lion's roar.
Each page crinkles like a gossip's jaw,
Words that stumble, yet leave us in awe.

Faded phrases chuckle in the breeze,
Worn words promise comfort, if you please.
Tripping over wisdom in honks and laughs,
Yet, finding gold in our silly gaffes.

Tattered scripts with stories galore,
Plot twists that no one could ignore.
Weathered pages hold treasures tight,
In quirky tales that burst with delight.

Words may be tired, yet spirits soar,
A chuckle or two never felt like a chore.
With every scratch, life scribbles its jest,
This chaotic script beats all the rest.

The Longing of the Lost Lyric

In the attic of thought, a tune goes missing,
Rhymes float around, but none are kissing.
A sprinkle of jests in forgotten notes,
Searching for melodies, like lost goats.

The chorus we crave slips through the pane,
Leaving us giggling in puzzled disdain.
Lines that once sparkled lie flat and bare,
Yet still, we riff on this comical air.

Lyrics once vibrant become faint and shy,
With every new stanza, we just wonder why.
Can verses grow legs and dance instead?
In this quirky search, who needs a thread?

Yet somehow, laughter finds its way,
In each off-key note, we've made our play.
For songs may fade, but joy we'll find,
In the silliness of the searching mind.

The Mirage of the Muse Meander

A flicker of thought, then poof, it's gone,
Kind of like catching a caffeinated dawn.
The muse dances round, wearing mismatched shoes,
Sparkling with chaos and potentially blues.

With every twist in this unpredictable chase,
Ideas tumble like a pie in the face.
Each moment a treasure, then poof! It's done,
Laughter erupts at the unwritten pun.

The muse thinks it's funny to vanish at night,
Yet returns with her giggles, what a sight!
A mirage of inspiration, a wild charade,
Notebook in hand, we're too fun to fade.

In this merry chase, with jests our aim,
Crafting good humor in a fickle game.
Though the muse may flee, our spirits remain,
In the jest of creation, laughter's our gain.

In Search of Elusive Words

Upon my desk the paper lies,
With empty lines that mock my cries.
A rhyme escapes, it dances near,
Yet slips away, it's gone, I fear.

I chase it down, that fleeting thought,
With silly schemes and battles fought.
The scribbles sprawl like playful pets,
Each straying thought, a gamble, bets.

In coffee cups and muffin crumbs,
In frantic leaps my mind succumbs.
With every smile, a joke I write,
But words evade, like birds in flight.

Yet laughter echoes in my quest,
For every fail, a jest is best.
The pursuit of lines, a joyful jest,
In searching hard, I find the rest.

The Poet's Pondering Pause

I sit and ponder in my chair,
With furrowed brow and tousled hair.
The words elude, a sneaky team,
They giggle soft, disrupt my dream.

What is the verse? What's the right twist?
A sonnet's imminent, I insist!
But on this page, they stutter, halt,
And leave me here to ponder, vault.

The clock ticks loud, a taunting beat,
My mind's a dance of stubborn feet.
I scribble nonsense, rhyme a fruit,
In every line, a silly hoot.

Yet joy erupts in every flub,
Each pause a step, a happy grub.
For in this chaos, mirth ignites,
A poet's pause turns wrong to rights.

The Dilemma of the Draft

A draft so bold, it winks at me,
With crafty lines that call for glee.
But each new word, a daunting task,
I question now, what's this I ask?

The phrases tangle, twist, and shout,
As I wrestle logic, flip about.
Chasing rhymes like a puppy's chase,
In circles round, it's quite the race.

Is it a sonnet, should it rhyme?
Or should I break all rules this time?
The mess I make, it piles on high,
Yet laughter lives where riddles lie.

In drafts I find my pure delight,
Although I scream with all my might.
For every word that goes awry,
A chuckle lifts, oh me, oh my!

Trapped in Temporal Tension

Time ticks by, a playful tease,
As I sit still, my mind a breeze.
Each second laughs, it runs away,
   While I remain, in disarray.

A sonnet waits, a dance unspun,
Yet all I hear is time's soft pun.
My thoughts are weights, as clocks do glide,
   With every tick, they slip, subside.

To rhyme or not, the question's there,
While time, my foe, pretends to care.
In frantic whirl, I throw my lines,
   Yet all I catch are tangled signs.

But in this spin, I find the fun,
As laughter breaks the clockwork run.
For moments lost in playful woes,
   Create the seeds where humor grows.

Echoes of Lost Verses

In a world of rhymes, I lost my way,
The meter slipped like butter on a tray.
Thoughts tangled like a cat in a ball,
Words danced around, yet I can't recall.

The pen now laughs, mocking my plight,
As I search for lines that seem just right.
The paper sighs, it won't cooperate,
Each word I choose just seals my fate.

I scribble furiously, hoping for gold,
But find only riddles, and stories untold.
The muse takes a nap, oh what a shame,
Leaving me here feeling quite lame.

So here I sit, in poetic despair,
Trying to catch thoughts, just floating in air.
Perhaps if I rhyme "cheese" with "bees",
These echoes of loss might float on the breeze.

Quandaries of a Bard

The bard set out with a quill in his hand,
To pen a great tale of love, oh so grand.
But words turned to mush, like bread gone stale,
Each thought a fish that would flounder and flail.

Should I rhyme "cat" with "flat" or "bat"?
The options are endless, I'm lost in chat.
The fates conspire to twist my quill,
As every new notion gives me a thrill.

Oh what's that sound? A tumbleweed rolls,
Imagine my fate when it chortles and tolls!
An audience waits with bated breath,
For a sonnet about love or perhaps death.

Yet here I write and trip over rhyme,
Wishing for structure, just one little chime.
With giggles and grumbles, I dance on my page,
In the quandary of a bard—a humorous stage.

Musings in Metered Silence

In silence I muse, with lines in my head,
Like grains of rice spilling out of a shed.
The meter is missing, it's off like a clock,
Words hide in the nooks, like a sly little fox.

I ponder on topics that dance in the dark,
But all that I get is a sarcastic spark.
The rhyme scheme eludes like a butterfly's flight,
Perhaps I should just stop, or take a short flight.

Oh, what is a poet without clever phrase?
A riddle, a jester, caught in a daze.
With lines that run wild like a wind-swept kite,
Shall I call it a day or continue this blight?

In musings of silence, I giggle and grin,
For nothing's quite fun as the chaos within.
Each stumble on syllables turns into cheer,
Creating a jingle that the stars can hear.

A Rhyme on the Tip of the Tongue

A rhyme I've forgotten, it danced on my tongue,
But vanished like echoes in songs never sung.
Words flit like fairies, just out of my grasp,
Leaving me tangled in thoughts that clasp.

What was that phrase? Was it "egg" with "leg"?
No, that won't do, it needs more of a beg.
I search through the weeds of my jumbled brain,
Hoping for clarity, but all I find is rain.

The clock ticks away as I churn and I stew,
Laughing at myself for the trouble I do.
My pen shakes in hand, but I carry the fight,
To catch those lost rhymes that giggle in flight.

With humor in mind, I can't help but sing,
Of the woes of a poet and the joy that it brings.
So here's to the chase, the missed and the fun,
For laughter and whimsy are never quite done.

The Art of Elusive Expression

In a garden of words, I plant my seeds,
But the alphabet weeds kill all my needs.
With a pen in my hand, I dance with despair,
A jumbled bouquet, both ugly and rare.

Each line I compose, a riddle untold,
Like socks in the dryer, they vanish, I'm sold.
I chase after phrases that run like the breeze,
Laughing at laughter; it's all just a tease.

The rhymes play hide-and-seek without any care,
I scribble and doodle, but find no affair.
Each stanza a puzzle, a jigsaw unmade,
Where's the punchline? Oh wait, is that my upgrade?

Yet, amid this chaos, I giggle and sigh,
For every misstep makes me want to fly.
So here's to the verses that play games with me,
With a wink and a grin, they set my mind free.

Shadows of a Forgotten Rhyme

In the attic of thought, my ideas get stuck,
Like old dusty boxes, full of bad luck.
I search for a couplet, a phrase I can hum,
But it dances away, saying, 'Not today, chum!'

With shadows of shadows, I stumble around,
Tripping on meter, I fall to the ground.
Each word is a ghost, haunting my confused mind,
A chuckle from failure, so silly, yet kind.

I chase after rhythms that giggle and tease,
Like kittens with yarn, they do as they please.
I write and erase, a comedic display,
With an audience of crickets that join in the fray.

So here's to the banter of verses gone wrong,
Where awkward's the melody, laughter's the song.
In the shadows I play, a poet amiss,
But the jest of my journey is pure comic bliss.

Crafting in the Void

In a cavern of silence, I ponder and toil,
With thoughts like mud puddles, deep in the soil.
I sketch out my dreams, but they giggle and flee,
Like jelly on toast, they just won't agree.

Each verse I attempt, a grand comedic flop,
An epic unfolding that never will stop.
I juggle with metaphors, they slip through my hands,
Leaving me breathless in my empty lands.

The ink spills in chaos, a wild, sweet mess,
With laughter erupting from this lovely stress.
I pen down my thoughts, will they stick or they fly?
A circus of whimsy, a spark in the sky.

Still, I revel in madness, embrace the absurd,
For humor's the treasure tucked deep in each word.
In the void of my craft, a silly delight,
Turns the mundane to magic, in the softest twilight.

The Dilemma of Daunting Muses

My muses have vanished, they're off on a spree,
Chasing clouds when they promised to stick with me.
I shout at the sky, but they giggle in flight,
A game of tag played in the warm, sunny light.

Each thought is a tease, a glove without a match,
An out-of-reach cookie hung high from the latch.
I reach for the moments they cleverly kept,
But they wink and decay like the rhymes that I've wept.

Like chairs in a dance hall, they spin out of sight,
They mock my attempts to get words to take flight.
I stumble on silence, a punchline confused,
And laughter rings clear as I muse, feeling bruised.

Yet here in this riddle, I find a sweet charm,
For each awkward twist brings its delightful alarm.
In this dance with my muses, I stumble, I play,
Creating a comedy in my own quirky way.

The Weight of Words Unspoken

In silence I sit with my pen in hand,
The paper stares back, just a desert land.
Thoughts tumble and trip, like a clown on the street,
But alas, they escape on invisible feet.

I frown at the ink that refuses to flow,
It teases my mind with a glimmering glow.
Like a cake with no frosting, it's bland and it's bare,
And I'm left here to ponder in blank, empty air.

How can I find those elusive little gems,
Hiding like ducks, in a row of bright stems?
A word here, a phrase there, I try to recall,
Yet all that comes trickling is nothing at all.

But laughter resounds in the chaos I face,
For even in silence, there's humor and grace.
I'll chuckle at nothing, with joy in my chest,
For words may be weighty, but fun is the best!

Chasing the Chimeras of Creativity

Chasing my thoughts like a dog on a run,
They zig and they zag, and they're hardly any fun.
I chase them with rhythm, but they bounce away,
Leaving me standing with naught left to say.

Imagination dances, a sprite on a lark,
But when I reach out, it just leaves a mark.
"Come back!" I implore, as it winks and it twirls,
Making me trip on my own silly swirls.

There's humor in trying to catch a wild thought,
Like fishing for air, it's a battle well fought.
With giggles of joy, I embrace the absurd,
For chasing chimeras is simply the word!

And so I keep leaping through nonsense and glee,
All while the chimeras just laugh at me.
In this funny pursuit of the whims of the mind,
I'll treasure the laughter, the best that I find.

Bound by the Blankness of the Page

A canvas so white, it's an artist's nightmare,
No strokes or no scribbles, just a breath of fresh air.
I tap on the surface, expecting it's fate,
But it chuckles at me, and I start to berate.

It's like having a dance without any feet,
Or a party of friends without any treat.
The lines of my thoughts, like fish in a stream,
Are slippery sayings, dissolving my dream.

Yet I sit here amused at the standstill before,
A battle of wits with the white paper's score.
Each crease tells a story, each flicker a tale,
But the blankness unravels my brain like a snail.

So I chuckle along, let the weirdness unfold,
For laughter through struggle is purest of gold.
In this quiet conundrum, I find a bright spark,
The page may be empty, but it tickles me stark!

The Storm Before the Stillness

In my mind's eye, there's a ruckus and roar,
As ideas collide, and the creativity soars.
It's thunder and lightning, a dramatic parade,
But soon all the chaos will probably fade.

Like a tempest of thoughts swirling round in my head,
They argue and bicker, but none will be said.
The calm's just a prelude, a joke that's unkind,
For every great answer, there's a storm I must find.

So I build tiny castles of fancy and flights,
While giggles erupt through the troubled delights.
Each wacky idea becomes part of the fun,
Till the calm right before me turns into a pun.

And as laughter rains down like a sweet summer breeze,
I embrace all the nonsense with joyful unease.
For the storm may pass softly, but laughter will last,
As I dance through the silliness, present and past!

Threads of Thought Tangled

In a web of yarn, my musings twirl,
Like spaghetti thrown, a chaotic swirl.
Each thought a noodle, slippery and bright,
I trip on my brain while chasing the light.

The puns get stuck, like fluff on a chair,
As I laugh at my mess, with nobody there.
Chasing my shadows, I stumble and fall,
Who knew inspiration could be such a brawl?

Lost in the maze where the ideas play,
They giggle and dance, then run away.
I pluck at the strings, trying to untie,
Each thought that escapes makes me wonder why.

Yet through all the knots, I find a new rhyme,
A treasure of giggles buried in time.
For tangled or clear, it's all just a game,
And laughter remains, the heart of the fame.

The Yearning for a Unified Voice

Voices collide, like pots in a stew,
Each bubbling thought has a flavor anew.
I mix up my metaphors, toss in some zest,
But harmony's recipe is still a great test.

In a choir of cats, I'm the odd little bird,
Singing off-key to each silly word.
I'm yearning for chorus, yet humming alone,
In this symphony's chaos, I've built my own throne.

The melody hiccups, then starts to run wild,
Like a toddler's tantrum with thoughts unreconciled.
I cackle at quips that just won't make sense,
As I dance in the rain, my sanity tense.

Yet laughter ignites, a flame in the dark,
As we bumble through verses, we find our own spark.
Though voices may clash in a raucous delight,
The beauty of chaos is our joy in the fight.

A Desert of Distant Ideas

Wandering dry sands of forgotten dreams,
Ideas flicker like mirages in beams.
I chase after whispers that flit on the breeze,
But they vanish like grains, escaping with ease.

In this vast wasteland of thoughts far away,
I talk to the cacti, they have much to say.
Each cactus a sage, with thorns for a coat,
I ponder their wisdom with nothing to quote.

A tumbleweed rolls, bringing giggles and sighs,
It's the only companion, a friend in disguise.
We laugh at the distance, the sun's blazing rays,
As we stumble through dryness, lost in a daze.

Yet sometimes a spark ignites in the sand,
An idea worth chasing, a thought close at hand.
And in this desert, absurdly I see,
That laughter's the oasis this journey can be.

The Drawbridge of Daring Diction

In a fortress of words, I raise up the gate,
With barbs on my tongue and wit that's so great.
I joust with my phrases, a knight in the fray,
Ready to duel with each word that might stray.

My vocabulary clangs, a raucous parade,
Like squirrels with swords in a silly charade.
I march on this bridge where the daring equip,
To conquer each sentence and never to trip.

But oh, what a battle, this game I design,
As I fumble and bumble, I'm searching for wine.
For every grand statement that's meant to impress,
There's laughter that echoes, a humorous mess.

Yet as I descend from my eloquent throne,
I find it's not bravado that makes it my own.
In the kingdom of words, we dance and rejoice,
For the laughter that's shared is the true, balanced voice.

Breathless in Blank Pages

In the midst of my writing spree,
The paper glares back at me.
Words escape like a sudden sneeze,
I'm stuck here, if you please.

With coffee cups piling high,
I wonder if I should just cry.
Such brilliant thoughts, where did they go?
Like lost socks in a laundry show.

The clock ticks in a mocking way,
As I ponder how to convey.
A rhyme that dances on the page,
But all I've got is writer's rage.

Oh, muse, where are you tonight?
Filling my brain with nonsense delight.
Help me weave this tangled thread,
Before I find a snack instead.

A Sonnet's Silent Grief

Quill in hand and thoughts a-flutter,
But all that comes out is a stutter.
Each line feels more like a chore,
I've got writer's block at the core.

In my mind, great verses twirl,
Like a dizzy dance in a whirl.
Yet here I sit, the page stays bare,
Wondering why I even dare.

The rhymes elude, like cats at play,
I scribble nonsense in dismay.
Oh, muse of mine, have you fled?
Your absence weighs upon my head.

A sonnet's goal, oh so sublime,
Instead I'm caught in a mime.
With laughter, I wrestle this plight,
And hope for better words tonight.

The Labyrinth of Lingering Lines

In a maze where words turn to dust,
I search for inspiration, I must.
Each corner leads to more dead ends,
While my mind plays tricks like old friends.

A metaphor hides behind a wall,
Should I give up? Not at all!
With thoughts tangled like a yarn ball,
I chase them down the echoing hall.

Like a jester in this somber game,
With laughter, I try to light the flame.
But the lines just giggle and dance away,
Leaving me here, in disarray.

Oh sweet pen, what do you say?
Shall we twist and tumble today?
In this labyrinth we will play,
Until the dawn breaks out of gray.

Ink Stains of an Incomplete Thought

With ink stains sprawled across my wrist,
I ponder ideas that've been missed.
A thought so grand, or was it small?
It slipped away, I heed the call.

My notebook laughs, a spiteful tease,
As I scribble furiously, hoping to please.
But all the words seem out of touch,
What was so clever, now not much.

Page after page, a tangled maze,
In this funny little writing craze.
I search for meaning with lemonade,
And pray this writer's funk will fade.

So here I sit, a poet, lost,
But still I write, despite the cost.
With every drop of ink I learn,
That laughter's still my finest turn.

Haunted by the Hushed Harmonies

In stillness, whispers play a prank,
They seem to laugh, yet smell of blank.
A tune that teases, hides and gleams,
In the corners of forgotten dreams.

I chase these notes, a jolly fool,
With every step, I lose my cool.
They giggle, twirl, then run away,
Leaving me here to misplay the day.

My thoughts like butterflies, on a spree,
But every net's an empty plea.
I scribble lines, a silly dance,
These words elude my wild romance.

Yet still I grin, despite the jest,
For laughter shines—it feels the best.
A haunted tune, a playful ghost,
In harmony's chains, I live, I boast!

Echoes of Unexpressed Emotion

A thud, a bump, in the heart's deep halls,
Echoes of laughter against the walls.
But where's the joy? The punchline's fled,
Left me to ponder what should be said.

I send a text, oh, what a game,
To express a thought, how absurdly lame!
With every tap, new fears arise,
What if I text and there's no replies?

A dance of words, none knows the steps,
I trip and tumble in verbal preps.
These emotions—like jigsaw bits,
Refuse to fit, they play in skits.

Yet laughter waits in the awkward space,
A chuckle's worth, my saving grace.
For in this odd, elusive cheer,
I find the joy of being here.

The Heavy Burden of Blankness

A weighty void sits on my muse,
My thoughts depart, they refuse to choose.
Each page lies bare, a solemn face,
Where words should frolic, in endless race.

I seek inspiration—it plays so sly,
Like a cheeky bird, it flies on by.
Each scribbled line feels like a chore,
My pencil sighs, a heartfelt bore.

Friends offer prompts, with glee they say,
"Just write a sonnet! It's a great way!"
But every time I beckon the thought,
I find a plot that's all for naught.

So I embrace this heavy plight,
In laughter's grip, I take to flight.
For hidden here, within the strain,
There's joy in jest, a merry gain.

The Veil Cast by Void

A shroud of silence wraps my brain,
Each thought escapes like drops of rain.
A veil so thick, it plays the tease,
Within its folds, my musings freeze.

I poke and prod, I lift and pry,
In hopes of finding what went awry.
Yet all I grasp is empty air,
A playful jest, this void I bear.

In shadows lurk the giggles bright,
Laughter flutters, just out of sight.
With each failed attempt, the joy unfolds,
In silliness, the heart upholds.

So let the void be my playful hall,
In the dance of words, I rise and fall.
For in this veil, I'll sow my cheer,
And find the fun in every fear.

Encounters with Unfulfilled Rhythms

In the garden of thoughts, I pluck a rhyme,
But the words slip and slide, losing their time.
Napping on paper, they refuse to wake,
Chasing gaps where verses break.

Laughter bubbles, a playful tease,
Puns and puns dance in the breeze.
With each line I write, giggles arise,
As my muse hides behind clever disguise.

With a flourish, I draw, but what do I see?
A turtle on stilts or a cat in a tree?
Each image a puzzle, a riddle so round,
Yet here I am, just spinning around.

Oh, the challenge of crafting this jest,
Beneath all the stumbles, I'm put to the test.
Still, I keep laughing, refusing to pout,
For a funny old poem is what it's about.

The Poet's Paralyzing Plight

A block of silence in my mind's busy street,
Where words play hide-and-seek, that's no treat.
Pen in hand, I circle, a lost little bee,
Buzzing toward realms of sweet poetry.

Yet the clock just ticks, with a mocking chime,
As I stare at blankness, wasting my prime.
Every thought a hiccup, every rhyme a cringe,
What's left of my cleverness? I hardly cringe.

Friends suggest tea or a walk in the sun,
But I stay glued here, my war just begun.
A duel with stanzas, a battle with rhyme,
Sending my sanity on a steep climb.

But lo and behold, a giggle escapes,
At the thought of my struggle in mismatched capes.
In the realm of the poets, I do find my place,
Even if it's just to laugh at my face.

Images in a Desert of Words

In a desert of phrases, dry as a bone,
I search for an oasis, feeling alone.
Cacti of couplets prick at my thoughts,
Each bloom a reminder of battles I've fought.

Scorpions sting as I wrestle with prose,
While mirages of metaphors tantalize those.
I chase after whispers of eloquent streams,
But they vanish like smoke, dissolving my dreams.

There's laughter in speaking where silence concedes,
A playful escape from the serious needs.
I scribble with glee, then giggles abound,
For what's lost in the desert can be joyfully found.

So I dance with my shadows, I tap and I twirl,
In this land of confusion, my thoughts all unfurl.
With a chuckle and wink, I'll keep up the fight,
In my desert of words, I'll find joy and delight.

Echoing the Unformed

In the hall of echoes, whispers collide,
Thoughts tumble and fumble, nowhere to hide.
Each notion a ripple, a giggle unwound,
As I chase after sounds that just spin around.

A cacophony calls, but oh, what a jest,
Each proclamation, a humorous quest.
With every missed rhyme, I laugh 'til I cry,
For perfection in lyrics is just a sly lie.

In this echo chamber, my mind plays a tune,
Like a cat playing jazz on a watery moon.
I capture the chaos, let it whirl through the air,
As laughter, not order, becomes my affair.

So here's to the echoes that bounce and rebound,
To the humorous rhymes lost behind each sound.
With a skip in my heart and a smile on my face,
I'll dance through the echoes, my own silly space.

Enigmas in the Emptiness of Expression

Words wander round like lost sheep,
Hoping to find a rhyme so deep.
Each thought gets tangled in its own twist,
As ideas swirl in an empty mist.

Laughter echoes in every blank page,
Ideas dance like a playful sage.
But when the punchline is nowhere near,
I chuckle, then shed a silly tear.

Obstacles on the Path to Prose

Running in circles, my mind's in a jam,
Search for a topic, but oh, how I scram!
Puns and jokes pop like bubbles in soda,
The page stays blank despite the grand quota.

Stumbling over a misplaced jest,
The humor is there, but I feel so stressed.
Barriers rise like a great wall of cheese,
Tasting the words, but they never appease.

The Search for Spirited Syntax

Syntax sneaks away, like a runaway cat,
Grasping at letters, I ponder and chat.
Like a magician, I try to conjure,
But all that appears is a sad little grunge.

Rhythms trot lightly, but trip on a beat,
I laugh at the dance of this literary feat.
Words on parade, yet they all seem shy,
Where'd all the good lines go? Oh my, oh my!

Labored Lines to Lasting Lyrics

Crafting a line with sweat on my brow,
Each word is a puzzle, but I don't know how.
Twists and turns, like a rollercoaster spree,
I scream with both joy and a tinge of plea.

Some lines are gems, while others just stink,
A cacophony of chaos in ink.
But in every struggle there's laughter to find,
Each silly mishap, forever entwined.

Hurdles in the Harmony of Haiku

Oh, write a haiku, how hard can it be?
Just three little lines, one, two, then three.
But syllables trip, like a dance on the floor,
Now I'm laughing at words that I thought I'd explore.

The nature is quiet, yet my thoughts go wild,
A bird chirps a tune, but my pen has reviled.
It's a puzzle, a game, with no sense of play,
Why does writing simple feel like a ballet?

The tall grass is swaying, my mind's in a knot,
I scribble and doodle, but what have I got?
The sun's shining bright, but my ink's running dry,
I guess I'll just sit here and give it a sigh.

Yet in this great mess, I will still find a cheer,
For laughter and chaos, they make it all clear.
Each word that I clutch, it's a bump on the ride,
Creating the fun that I won't try to hide.

A Labored Love for Language

Oh, language, dear love, you make me so mad,
Your grammar's a maze, your rules are so bad.
With commas and clauses, I'm chasing my tail,
What's "who" and what's "whom?" I'm destined to fail.

I try to be witty, I rhyme and I scheme,
But finding the right words feels like a bad dream.
Alliteration dances, but my tongue's in a twist,
I'm lost in my thoughts, like a ball on a mist.

Each verse that I craft seems to trip on a shoe,
While I'm sprinkling puns like they're glitter, who knew?
My metaphors bumble and similes pout,
Yet still I persist, with a grin and a shout.

So here's to the love that's a labor so grand,
I'll wrestle with words, I will take my bold stand.
In all the confusion, I'll chuckle and sigh,
For laughter in language makes reason go by.

Pages Unturned in the Poetic Pursuit

A poet sits idle, with papers all scattered,
Staring at screens, with ideas all battered.
Each draft that I write feels like running a race,
But pages unturned always give me a space.

I flip through the chapters, my thoughts come and go,
With metaphors hiding just out of the flow.
The coffee is cold, and my muse took a flight,
Where's the ink for my heart? It has vanished from sight.

They say that it's easy, just scribble and cheer,
But I'm stuck on a line that won't make it quite clear.
Each word that I type feels like playing a game,
I laugh at the struggle, it's never the same.

Yet I dance on my fears like a clown on a stage,
With joy in my heart, I will turn every page.
For each little hiccup, each stumble and fall,
Turns the awkward to art, the best joke of all.

The Desperation of a Deadlocked Dream

In the land of ideas, I'm lost at a door,
A dream that was grand now lies flat on the floor.
I tug on the handle, but it won't budge free,
Each thought I once cherished has run off with glee.

Oh, what did I plan when the sun filled my head?
A sonnet of wonders, now silenced in dread.
The clock ticks so slow, every second a joke,
As visions of brilliance drift up in the smoke.

So I'll grab my silly hat, and dance in the gloom,
Creating a circus from the chaos of doom.
With laughter as medicine for fears I can't see,
I'll tip my top hat and just let it all be.

For dreams that feel stuck are just taking their time,
In the land of the quirky, I'll still find my rhyme.
And in every deadlock, there's a punchline to find,
Where giggles and chuckles await for the mind.

The Challenge of Untamed Lines

My pen awoke, a flirt with fate,
Yet every phrase has gone on holiday.
I scribble dreams on a paper plate,
But all I catch is a stylish disarray.

The muse skipped town on the midnight train,
Leaving me here to tattle and whine.
My thoughts parade, but all in vain,
As rhymes retreat like a shy divine.

Each word feels lost, like changing trains,
As I chase shadows beneath the sun.
Lines tangled up in a tangled chain,
Where wit and whimsy seem to shun.

I laugh aloud at this silly plight,
A sonnet lost in a game of charades.
With every twist, I revel in slight,
Crafting nonsense in poetic cascades.

Fragments of a Fading Muse

The muse once danced in my cluttered mind,
With graceful steps and a wink of cheer.
Now she's a ghost, too hard to find,
Hiding behind each forgotten sphere.

I search the clouds for inspiration,
Only to find a stray kite instead.
Lines floating high in wild creation,
But all I write are things I dread.

The ink spills forth like a playful tide,
Yet laughter echoes where logic wanes.
I pen the tales of the greats who've tried,
But end up stuck in their comic chains.

With every stutter, the quill does tease,
Crafting humor from each teetering thought.
A merry dance that aims to please,
As fragments of muses twist and knot.

Struggles Beneath the Quill

Oh, the quill grips tight, a reluctant friend,
As I grapple with thoughts that don't come alive.
Each word feels like it's refusing to bend,
While I roar with laughter at this failed strive.

In desperate haste, I chase the muse,
Like a child chasing after a runaway kite.
But she's playing tricks, and I'm just confused,
Tripping on rhymes in a whimsical fight.

My notebook fills with doodles and jest,
Attempts at sonnets that just fall flat.
Each page a riddle, a jumbled quest,
With humor stuck in a poet's hat.

If only the quill could spill out some glee,
Instead of this mess I venture to frame.
As laughter spills wide, will it comfort me?
This battle of wits is a silly game.

Tangles in the Tapestry of Verse

Tangled threads of a jumbled weave,
Each word a knot that refuses to flow.
I reach for brilliance, but oh, I grieve,
For every idea feels shy and low.

The tapestry frays as I strive and pull,
Gleeful chaos in every line drawn.
Moments of mirth, a jest so dull,
As I tiptoe on rhymes from dusk till dawn.

Yet through the twists where confusion reigns,
I find a laugh nestled in the fray.
For every typo that warps and remains,
Becomes a punchline I can display.

So here I stand, with my tangled plot,
A jester caught in a merry ruse.
For laughter will bubble in each silly jot,
In the tapestry woven from my muse.

Whispers of Unwritten Dreams

A pen in hand, I start to write,
But all my thoughts just take to flight.
The page is blank, a ghostly grin,
Where verses hide, and laughter spins.

I chase a rhyme, it slips away,
A hide-and-seek with words at play.
A sonnet's form now feels so bold,
But here I stand, just feeling cold.

Ideas bubble, pop and burst,
I write them down, but that is cursed.
A haiku sneaks, a limerick dives,
In uncharted waters, nonsense thrives.

So here I sit, with humor's flair,
Unwritten dreams float in the air.
In laughter's grasp, my pen does dance,
To write my fate, I miss my chance.

The Poet's Puzzled Heart

With every beat, my heart's in knots,
Amidst the rhymes and twisted thoughts.
I juggle lines, a curious show,
As words evade, they scurry low.

Each stanza starts, then takes a break,
A playful tease, a tiny quake.
My mind a maze with paths obscured,
In quest of phrases, badly lured.

A couplet teases, then it slips,
The comedic timing, tightens grips.
An ode to chaos, here I stand,
With laughter as my guiding hand.

And though I fumble, lose my way,
In silly verse, I choose to play.
A poet's heart, though puzzled still,
Finds joy in nonsense, what a thrill!

In Search of Stanzas Unspoken

In empty rooms, the echoes sigh,
Where verses linger, then just fly.
Ambitious thoughts elude my grip,
Yet comedy's a steady ship.

A lyric lost, like socks in wash,
I laugh it off, then giggle posh.
With metaphors that hide and seek,
My lines grow shy, and subtly peek.

A sonnet's charm leads me astray,
As punchlines dance, then run away.
I scribble fast, don't lose the fun,
In silly language, I shall run.

Each stanza sought becomes a jest,
In playful search, I find my quest.
The laughter rings, my words take flight,
In whimsical prose, I find delight.

When Words Defy the Page

Oh, words that play the great escape,
From parchment prison, what a shape!
They twist and twirl, then jump about,
In every corner, there's a shout.

Metaphors that dare to tease,
Slippery phrases, filled with ease.
I pen them down, yet still they flee,
A clever trick, they laugh at me.

With humor's lens, I view my plight,
The rhymes that mock me in the night.
A silly grin, as I partake,
In nonsense songs my heart will make.

So let them dance, those words so spry,
In whimsical worlds, they surely fly.
In laughter's grip, I choose to play,
For joy resides where words delay.

Labors of Lyrical Longing

My pen once danced with joy so bright,
 But now it scribbles, tries to write.
 With coffee spills and papers torn,
 I laugh at rhymes that feel forlorn.

Each word a puzzle, lost in space,
 A jigsaw mad, yet I embrace.
The mismatched socks of sonnet quest,
 A carnival of lines, a silly jest.

I search for rhythm, seek a scheme,
 But tripping on my own wild dream.
 The verses tumble like a clumsy cat,
 With playful grace, I muse on that.

In every stumble, joy unspools,
 A hearty laugh, I've learned the rules.
 For writing's joy is found in fun,
 Each line a giggle, clever run.

The Paradox of a Paused Pen

Oh, woe betide my ink-filled friend,
It sits so still, the hours blend.
A paradox of art and strife,
A pen that fights for literary life.

It teases thoughts, then holds them tight,
It's like a cat in search of light.
A noodle in a bowl, it sways,
As if to say, 'Write me today!'

With scratching noise, it starts to hum,
Yet silence steals away the fun.
A comedy of errors, I compose,
A script for laughter, who truly knows?

The words like marbles scatter wide,
But in the chaos, dreams abide.
Let's cheer for pens that sit and sway,
For every pause brings humor's play.

Forbidden Flavors of Language

I dipped my pen in coffee grounds,
An espresso shot of quirky sounds.
The flavors mixed in funny ways,
While rhymes, like candy, lead astray.

Syllables like sprinkles, a riotous mess,
With hints of joy and some distress.
The language twists, like taffy, sweet,
Each poem's taste, a wild treat.

I pluck the berries from the verse,
Some taste like joy, while others curse.
Cooking lines with whimsy bold,
A feast for thoughts, or so I'm told.

Yet even as each word collides,
I savor every twist that bides.
For in this kitchen, chaos reigns,
The fun of writing never wanes.

The Legend of the Lost Lines

Beneath the stars, the lines took flight,
A mischievous dance in the moonlight.
They whispered tales of joy and rue,
A legend formed in shades of blue.

But oh! The pen, it slipped away,
Leaving behind a jumbled stray.
A pot of gold or just a tease?
This quest for words, a comical breeze.

Each lost line hides in laughter's glow,
Where silly thoughts begin to flow.
I chase the echoes of their glee,
A frantic quest, it seems to me.

But in the chaos, wonder thrives,
A laughter moves, and joy arrives.
For every line that tumbles down,
Is just a chance to wear a crown.

The Hesitant Heart of a Wordsmith

A quill in hand, my mind takes flight,
Words dance around, but none feel right.
I scribble once, I scribble twice,
Yet all I write is cold as ice.

A rhyme escapes, it trips and falls,
I chase it down, it laughs and sprawls.
The page is blank, my muse is shy,
Oh, where is inspiration? My, oh my!

Each phrase I pen feels out of tune,
Like a cat meowing at the moon.
I chuckle soft, this jest so grand,
A wordsmith's fate, a tired hand.

But joy does sneak in with a rhyme,
Even if it takes me time.
So here I sit, with dreams of verse,
Perhaps I'm cursed, or maybe just terse.

Secrets Shrouded in Silence

In a library quiet, secrets dwell,
Books hold tales that they never tell.
Whispers of plot twist through the air,
While I just sit, mustering a stare.

A cover's bright, but the inside's gloom,
A vast expanse within a room.
Librarians chuckle, what's the delay?
I nod along with nothing to say.

Pages flutter like anxious birds,
What's worse, my fear or these absurd words?
I seek a plot, but find no thread,
Tracing the thoughts that dance in my head.

So here I ponder, laugh at fate,
Is this the life of an author's slate?
I'll turn these hushes into a song,
And laugh at how I've wandered wrong.

Unraveled Threads of Thought

Tangled yarns weave stories awry,
Each twist, a chance, I dare to try.
Yet every time, they come undone,
My clever lines begin to run.

A needle of wit, it feels so dull,
Each stitch I take is prone to lull.
A thought appears, but slips away,
Like a squirrel playing hide and sway.

Ideas shrink like socks in a wash,
What once seemed grand is now a quash.
My mind's a maze, a jester's game,
I search for sense, but find the same.

Yet in this chaos, laughter blooms,
Amid the jumble, joy consumes.
My tangled tales may cause some strife,
But here's to the laughter in this life!

The Conundrum of Conceptual Clarity

Thoughts collide in a vibrant mess,
Each idea feels like a game of chess.
The knight jumps here, the bishop sighs,
I seek the truth through comics and lies.

A moment of brilliance, a flash of light,
Then back to haze, like a feather in flight.
Do I write nonsense or something profound?
The answer's lost, floating around.

Logic's a riddle, a puzzle unspooled,
Yet here I am, forever a fool.
But laughter's my guide through this wacky maze,
As I scribble and wander in whimsical ways.

So cheers to the chaos, the fun we can find,
In a world where we all feel a bit blind.
We'll weave our truths in the quirkiest way,
Turning confusion into a hilarious play.

Caged in the Crucible of Creation

In the corner, ideas squawk,
Trapped in a cage of endless talk.
They flap and flap, never take flight,
While I just sit and stare at the light.

The pen heavy like a weighty ball,
My muse is on break, it's a no-call.
Words scatter like leaves in the breeze,
Oh, give me a break, or just a tease!

Each line feels like it needs a tune,
Doodle a sonnet, but it's all a cartoon.
Laughing at my own poetic plight,
As rhymes slip away into the night.

So here I am, with paper and pen,
Chasing the muse, when will it end?
Just a giggle at my tangled spree,
A comedy of errors, just let me be.

Frustrations in a Flickering Flame

The candle flickers, ideas fly,
Like fireflies dancing, oh my oh my!
Each flicker a thought, but they slip away,
Just out of reach, bright in dismay.

I wave my pen, it's a wand of sorts,
Casting spells for poetic retorts.
But all I get is a puff of smoke,
My clever lines, just a cruel joke.

A page full of doodles, no rhyme in sight,
I scribble a word, and it feels just right.
Then giggle as letters begin to misbehave,
Slipping like a greased pig, oh how they save!

With a wink and a smirk, I strike a pose,
Wishing for verses that rhythmically flows.
Yet laughter is now my best friend here,
As I chase down the muse without any fear.

The Quest for Quiet Inspiration

In the quest for quiet, I roam the page,
My brain's a circus, it's all the rage.
Clowns dance around, ideas jive,
But coherent thoughts? They seem to hide.

I close my eyes, seek a calm sea,
Yet the mind's a buzzing, unruly bee.
Words swarm and twist like a carnival ride,
As I laugh at the chaos that won't abide.

Each line bounces like a rubber ball,
Full of energy, but they always fall.
"Focus!" I shout, but the breeze just shushes,
I scribble a line, and that moment crushes.

But here's the twist in this playful game,
The quest for calm has become a funny name.
I'll take my jumbled lines with joy,
Who needs perfection? I'm just a coy.

Verses in a Virtual Void

In a digital space where echoes reside,
I type out my hopes, but the words just slide.
Pixels collide like fireflies bright,
Yet no sense is made, try as I might.

The screen mocks me with its cold, blank stare,
A virtual world, but I find it bare.
Each click of the keys sends out a plea,
For verses to come, like plucked from a tree.

Emails ding like poetry's bell,
Prompts from the void, but they never gel.
I laugh at the silence that fills up the air,
My jests echo back, but they seem unaware.

Still here I sit, in this pixel parade,
Crafting my words in the virtual shade.
A funny old dance, oh what a choice,
As I'm lost in the void, I still find my voice.

www.ingramcontent.com/pod-product-compliance
Lightning Source LLC
Chambersburg PA
CBHW071845160426
43209CB00003B/419